DO WE AGREE?

DO WE AGREE?

A DEBATE BETWEEN
G. K. CHESTERTON
AND
BERNARD SHAW
WITH
HILAIRE BELLOC
IN THE CHAIR

HASKELL HOUSE
Publishers of Scholarly Books
NEW YORK
1964

First Published 1928

HASKELL HOUSE PUBLISHERS LTD.
Publishers of Scarce Scholarly Books
280 LAFAYETTE STREET
NEW YORK, N. Y. 10012

Library of Congress Catalog Card Number: 65-15899

Standard Book Number 8383-0525-3

Printed in the United States of America

A PREFATORY NOTE

In justice to all concerned I feel it to be my duty to state frankly that this account of a public discussion between Mr. Chesterton and Mr. Shaw is something less than a verbatim report. But with some assistance from the debaters it has been possible to save enough from oblivion to justify publication.

C.P.

DO WE AGREE?

MR. BELLOC : I am here to take the chair in the debate between two men whom you desire to hear more than you could possibly desire to hear me. They will debate whether they agree or do not agree. From what I know of attempts at agreement between human beings there is a prospect of a very pretty fight. When men debate agreement between nations then you may be certain a disastrous war is on the horizon. I make an exception for the League of Nations, of which I know nothing. If the League of Nations could make a war it would be the only thing it ever has made.

I do not know what Mr. Chesterton is going to say. I do not know what Mr. Shaw is going to say. If I did I would not say it for them. I vaguely gather from what I have heard that they are going to try to discover a principle : whether men should be free to possess private means, as is Mr. Shaw, as is Mr. Chesterton ; or should be, like myself, an embarrassed person, a publishers' hack. I could tell them; but my mouth is shut. I am not allowed to say what I think. At any rate, they are going to debate this sort of thing. I know not what more to say. They are about to debate. You are about to listen. I am about to sneer.

MR. SHAW: Mr. Belloc, and Ladies and Gentlemen. Our subject this evening, " Do We Agree ? " was an inspiration of Mr. Chesterton's. Some of you might reasonably wonder, if we agree, what we are going to debate about. But I suspect that you do not really care much what we debate about provided we entertain you by talking in our characteristic manners.

The reason for this, though you may not know it—and it is my business to tell you— is that Mr. Chesterton and I are two madmen. Instead of doing honest and respectable work and behaving ourselves as ordinary citizens, we go about the world possessed by a strange gift of tongues—in my own case almost exclusively confined to the English language —uttering all sorts of extraordinary opinions for no reason whatever.

DO WE AGREE? 9

Mr. Chesterton tells and prints the most extravagant lies. He takes ordinary incidents of human life—commonplace middle-class life—and gives them a monstrous and strange and gigantic outline. He fills suburban gardens with the most impossible murders; and not only does he invent the murders but also succeeds in discovering the murderer who never committed the murders. I do very much the same sort of thing. I promulgate lies in the shape of plays; but whereas Mr. Chesterton takes events which you think ordinary and makes them gigantic and colossal to reveal their essential miraculousness, I am rather inclined to take these things in their utter commonplaceness, and yet to introduce among them outrageous ideas which scandalize the ordinary play-goer and send him away wondering whether he has been standing on his head all his life or whether I am standing on mine.

A man goes to see one of my plays and sits by his wife. Some apparently ordinary thing is said on the stage, and his wife says to him: " Aha ! What do you think of that ? " Two minutes later another apparently ordinary thing is said and the man turns to his wife and says to her: "Aha! What do *you* think of *that*?"

Curious, is it not, that we should go about doing these things and be tolerated and even largely admired for doing them? Of late years I might say that I have almost been reverenced for doing these things.

Obviously we are mad; and in the East we should be reverenced as madmen. The wisdom of the East says: "Let us listen to these men carefully; but let us not forget that they are madmen."

In this country they say "Let us listen to these amusing chaps. They are perfectly sane, which we obviously are not." Now there must be some reason for shewing us all this consideration. There must be some force in nature which. . . . .

> At this point the debate was interrupted by persistent knocking at the doors by ticket-holders who had, through some misunderstanding, been locked out. On the chairman's intervention the doors were opened, and order was restored. Mr. Shaw then proceeded:

Ladies and Gentlemen, I must go on

because, as you see, if I don't begin to talk everybody else does. Now I was speaking of the curious respect in which mad people are held in the East and in this country. What I was leading up to is this, that it matters very little on what points they differ: they have all kinds of aberrations which rise out of their personal circumstances, out of their training, out of their knowledge or ignorance. But if you listen to them carefully and find that at certain points they agree, then you have some reason for supposing that here the spirit of the age is coming through, and giving you an inspired message. Reject all the contradictory things they say and concentrate your attention on the things upon which they agree, and you may be listening to the voice of revelation.

You will do well to-night to listen attentively, because probably what is urging us to these utterances is not personal to ourselves but some conclusion to which all mankind is moving either by reason or by inspiration. The mere fact that Mr. Chesterton and I may agree upon any point may not at all prevent us from debating it passionately. I find that the people who fight me generally hold the very ideas I am trying to express. I do not know if it is because they resent the liberty I am taking or because they do not like the words I use or the twist of my mind; but they are the people who quarrel most with me.

You have at this moment a typical debate raging in the Press. You have a very pretty controversy going on in the Church of England between the Archbishop of Canterbury and the Bishop of Birmingham. I hope you have all read the admirable letter of the Archbishop of Canterbury. Everybody is pleased with that letter. It has the enormous virtue of being entirely good-humoured, of trying to make peace, of avoiding making mischief: a popular English virtue which is a credit to the English race. But it has another English quality which is a little more questionable, and that is the quality of being entirely anti-intellectual. The letter is a heartfelt appeal for ambiguity. You can imagine the Archbishop of Canterbury, if he were continuing the controversy in private, saying to the Bishop of Birmingham: " Now, my dear Barnes, let me recommend you to read that wonderful book, *The Pilgrim's*

Progress. Read the history of the hero, Christian, no doubt a very splendid fellow, and from the literary point of view the only hero of romantic fiction resembling a real man. But he is always fighting. He is out of one trouble into another. He is leading a terrible life. How different to that great Peacemaker, Mr. Facing-Both-Ways! Mr. Facing-Both-Ways has no history. Happy is the country that has no history; and happy, you may say, is the man who has no history; and Mr. Facing-Both-Ways in *The Pilgrim's Progress* is that man."

Bunyan, by the way, does not even mention Mr. Facing-Both-Ways' extraordinary historical feat of drafting the Twenty-seventh Article of the Church of England. There being some very troublesome people for Elizabeth to deal with—Catholics and Puritans, for instance, quarrelling about Transubstantiation—Mr. Facing-Both-Ways drafted an Article in two paragraphs. The first paragraph affirmed the doctrine of Transubstantiation. The second paragraph said it was an idle superstition. Then Queen Elizabeth was able to say "Now you are all satisfied; and you must all attend the Church of England. If you don't I will send you to prison."

But I am not for one moment going to debate the doctrine of Transubstantiation. I mention it only to shew, by the controversy between the Archbishop and the Bishop, that in most debates you will find two types of mind playing with the same subject. There is one sort of mind that I think is my own sort. I sometimes call it the Irish mind, as distinct from the English mind. But that is only to make the English and Irish sit up and listen. Spengler talks not of Irish and English minds, but of the Greek, or Grecian mind, and the Gothic mind—the Faustian mind as he, being a German, calls it. And in this controversy you find that what is moving Bishop Barnes is a Grecian dislike of not knowing what it is he believes, and on the other side a Gothic instinctive feeling that it is perhaps just as well not to know too distinctly. I am not saying which is the better type of mind. I think on the whole both of them are pretty useful. But I always like to know what it is I am preaching. It gets me into trouble in England, where people say, "Why go into these matters? Why do you want to think so

DO WE AGREE? 15

accurately and sharply?" I can only say that my head is built that way; but I protest that I do not claim any moral superiority because when I know what I mean the other people do not know what they mean, and very often do not know what I mean. And one subject on which I know what I mean is the opinion which has inevitably been growing up for the last hundred years or so, not so much an opinion as a revolt against the mis-distribution, the obviously monstrous and anomalous mis-distribution of wealth under what we call the capitalist system.

I have always, since I got clear on the subject of Socialism, said, Don't put in the foreground the nationalization of the means of production, distribution, and exchange: you will never get there if you begin with them. You have to begin with the question of the distribution of wealth.

The other day a man died and the Government took four and a half million pounds as death duty on his property. That man made all his money by the labour of men who received twenty-six shillings a week after years of qualifying for their work. Was that a reasonable distribution of wealth between them? We are all coming to the opinion that it was not reasonable. What does Mr. Chesterton think about it? I want to know, not only because of the public importance of his opinions, but because I have always followed Mr. Chesterton with extraordinary interest and enjoyment, and his assent to any view of mine is a great personal pleasure, because I am very fond of Mr. Chesterton.

Mr. Chesterton has rejected Socialism nominally, probably because it is a rather stupid word. But he is a Distributist, which means to-day a Redistributist. He has arrived by his own path at my own position. (Laughter.) I do not see why you should laugh: I cannot imagine anything more natural.

But now comes the question upon which I will ask Mr. Chesterton whether he agrees with me or not. The moment I made up my mind that the present distribution of wealth was wrong, the peculiar constitution of my brain obliged me to find out exactly how far it was wrong and what is the right distribution. I went through all the proposals ever made and through the arguments used in justification of the existing distribution; and I found they were utterly insensate and grotesque.

Eventually I was convinced that we ought to be tolerant of any sort of crime except unequal distribution of income. In organized society the question always arises at what point are we justified in killing for the good of the community. I should answer in this way. If you take two shillings as your share and another man wants two shillings and sixpence, kill him. Similarly, if a man accepts two shillings while you have two shillings and sixpence, kill him.

On the stroke of the hour, I ask Mr. Chesterton: " Do you agree with that ? "

MR. CHESTERTON : Ladies and gentlemen. The answer is in the negative. I don't agree with it. Nor does Mr. Shaw. He does not think, any more than I do, that all the people in this hall, who have already created some confusion, should increase the confusion by killing each other and searching each other's pockets to see whether there is half-a-crown or two shillings in them. As regards the general question, what I want to say is this: I should like to say to begin with that I have no intention of following Mr. Shaw into a discussion which would be very improper on my part on the condition of the Church of England. But since he has definitely challenged me on the point I will say—he will not agree—that Mr. Shaw is indeed a peacemaker and has reconciled both sides. For if the Archbishop is anti-intellectual, there will be nobody to pretend that the Bishop is intellectual.

A VOICE: Yes he is.

MR. CHESTERTON: Now as to the much more interesting question, about a much more interesting person than Bishop Barnes—I mean Mr. Shaw—I should like to say that in a sense I can agree with him, in which case he can claim a complete victory. This is not a real controversy or debate. It is an enquiry, and I hope a profitable and interesting enquiry. Up to a point I quite agree with him, because I did start entirely by agreeing with him, as many years ago I began by being a Socialist, just as he was a Socialist. Barring some difference of age we were in the same position. We grew in beauty side by side. I will not say literally we filled one home with glee: but I do believe we have filled a fair number of homes with glee. Whether

DO WE AGREE? 19

those homes included our own personal households it is for others to say. But up to a point I agreed with Mr. Shaw by being a Socialist, and I agreed upon grounds he has laid down with critical justice and lucidity, grounds which I can imagine nobody being such a fool as to deny : the distribution of property in the modern world is a monstrosity and a blasphemy. Thus I come to the important stage of the proceedings. I claim that I might agree with Mr. Shaw a step farther.

I have heard from nearly all the Socialists I have known, the phrase which Mr. Shaw has with characteristic artfulness avoided, a phrase which I think everyone will agree is common to collectivist philosophy, and the phrase is this : " that the means of production should be owned by the community." I ask you to note that phrase because it is really upon that that the whole question turns.

Now there is a sense in which I do agree with Mr. Bernard Shaw. There is a point up to which I would agree with that formula. So far as is possible under human conditions I should desire the community—or, as we used to call it in the old English language, the

Commons—to own the means of production. So far, I say, you have Mr. Bernard Shaw and me walking in fact side by side in the flowery meads. . . . But after that, alas ! a change takes place. The change is owing to Mr. Shaw's vast superiority, to his powerful intellect. It is not my fault if he has remained young, while I have grown in comparison wrinkled and haggard, old and experienced, and acquainted with the elementary facts of human life.

Now the first thing I want to note is this. When you say the community ought to own the means of production, what do you mean ? That is the whole point. There was a time when Mr. Shaw would probably have said in all sincerity that anything possessed by the State or the Government would be in fact possessed by the Commons : in other words, by the community. I do not wish to challenge Mr. Shaw about later remarks of his, but I doubt whether Mr. Shaw, in his eternal youth, still believes in democracy in that sense. I quite admit he has a more hopeful and hearty outlook in some respects, and he has even gone to the length of saying that if democracy will not do for mankind, perhaps it will do for some other creature different from mankind. He has almost proposed to invent a new animal, which might be supposed to live for 300 years. I am inclined to think that if Mr. Shaw lived for 300 years—and I heartily hope he will—I never knew a man more likely to do it—he would certainly agree with me. I would even undertake to prove it from the actual history of the last 300 years, but though I think it is probable I will not insist upon it. As a very profound philosopher has said, " You never can tell." And it may be that Mr. Shaw's immortal power of talking nonsense would survive even that 300 years and he would still be fixed in his unnatural theories in the matter.

Now I do not believe myself that Mr. Shaw thinks that the community, in the sense of that state which owns and rules, the thing that issues postage stamps and provides policemen, I do not believe he thinks that that community is now, at this moment, identical with the Commons, and I do not believe he really thinks that in his own socialistic state it would be identical. I am glad therefore that he has sufficient disordered common sense to perceive that, as a matter of fact, when you have vast systems, however just and however reasonably controlled, indirectly, by elaborate machinery of officials and other things, you do in fact find that those who rule are the few. It may be a good thing or a bad thing, but it is not true that all the people directly control. Collectivism has put all their eggs in one basket. I do not think that Mr. Shaw believes, or that anybody believes, that 12,000,000 men, say, carry the basket, or look after the basket, or have any real distributed control over the eggs in the basket. I believe that it is controlled from the centre by a few people. They may be quite right or quite necessary. A certain limit to that sort of control any sane man will recognize as necessary : it is not the same as the Commons controlling the means of production. It is a few oligarchs or a few officials who do in fact control all the means of production.

What Mr. Shaw means is not that all the people should control the means of production, but that the product should be distributed among the vast mass of the Commons, and that is quite a different thing. It is not controlling the means of production at all. If all the citizens had simply an equal share of the

DO WE AGREE? 23

income of the State they would not have any control of the capital. That is where G. K. Chesterton differs from George Bernard Shaw. I begin at the other end. I do not think that a community arranged on the principles of Distributism and on nothing else would be a perfect community. All admit that the society that we propose is more a matter of proportion and arrangement than a perfectly clear system in which all production is pooled and the result given out in wages. But what I say is this: Let us, so far as is possible in the complicated affairs of humanity, put into the hands of the Commons the control of the means of production—and real control. The man who owns a piece of land controls it in a direct and real sense. He really owns the means of production. It is the same with a man who owns a piece of machinery. He can use it or not use it. Even a man who owns his own tools or works in his own workshop, to that extent owns and controls the means of production.

But if you establish right in the middle of the State one enormous machine, if you turn the handle of that machine, and somebody, who must be an official, and therefore a ruler, distributes to everybody equally the food or whatever else is produced by that machine, no single one of any of these people receiving more than any other single person, but all equal fragments : that fulfils a definite ideal of equality, yet no single one of those citizens has any control over the means of production. They have no control whatever—unless you think that the prospect of voting about once every five years for Mr. Vanboodle—then a Socialist member—with the prospect that he will or will not make a promise to a political assembly or that he will or will not promise to ask a certain question which may or may not be answered—unless you think that by this means they possess control.

I have used the metaphor of the Collectivists of having all your eggs in one basket. Now there are men whom we are pleased to call bad eggs. They are not all of them in politics. On the other hand there are men who deserve the encomium of " good egg." There are, in other words, a number of good men and a number of bad men scattered among the commonwealth.

To put the matter shortly, I might say that all this theory of absolutely equal mechanical

DO WE AGREE? 25

distribution depends upon a sort of use of the passive mood. It is easy enough to say Property should be distributed, but who is, as it were, the subject of the verb? Who or what is to distribute? Now it is based on the idea that the central power which condescends to distribute will be permanently just, wise, sane, and representative of the conscience of the community which has created it.

That is what we doubt. We say there ought to be in the world a great mass of scattered powers, privileges, limits, points of resistance, so that the mass of the Commons may resist tyranny. And we say that there is a permanent possibility of that central direction, however much it may have been appointed to distribute money equally, becoming a tyranny. I do not think it would be difficult to suggest a way in which it could happen. As soon as any particular mob of people are behaving in some way which the governing group chooses to regard as anti-civic, supplies could be cut off easily with the approval of this governing group. You have only to call someone by some name like Bolshevist or Papist. You have only to tie some label on a set of people and the community will contentedly see these people starved into surrender.

We say the method to be adopted is the other method. We admit, frankly, that our method is in a sense imperfect, and only in that sense illogical. It is imperfect, or illogical, because it corresponds to the variety and differences of human life. Mr. Shaw is making abstract diagrams of triangles, squares, and circles; we are trying to paint a portrait, the portrait of a man. We are trying to make our lines and colours follow the characteristics of the real object. Man desires certain things. He likes a certain amount of liberty, certain kinds of ownership, certain kinds of local affection, and won't be happy without them.

There are a great many other things that might be said, but I think it will be clearer if I repeat some of the things we have already said.

I do in that sense accept the proposition that the community should own the means of production, but I say that the Commons should own the means of production, and the only way to do that is to keep actual hold upon land. Mr. Bernard Shaw proposes to distribute wealth. We propose to distribute power.

DO WE AGREE? 27

Mr. Shaw: I cannot say that Mr. Chesterton has succeeded in forcing a difference of opinion on me. There are, I suppose, at least some people in this room who have heard me orating on this platform at lectures of the Fabian Society, and they must have been considerably amused at Mr. Chesterton's attempt to impress upon me what income is. My main activity as an economist of late has been to try to concentrate the attention of my party on the fact not only that they must distribute income, but that there is nothing else to distribute.

We must be perfectly clear as to what capital is. I will tell you. Capital is spare money. And, of course, spare money means spare food. If I happen to have more of the means of subsistence than I can use, I may take that part that is unconsumed, and say to another man: "Let me feed you whilst you produce some kind of contraption that will facilitate my work in future." But when the man has produced it for me, the capital has all gone: there is nothing left for me or him to eat. If he has made me a spade I cannot eat that spade.

I have said I *may* employ my spare subsistence in this way; but I *must* employ it so because it will not keep: if nobody eats it, it will go rotten. The only thing to be done with it is to have it promptly consumed. All that remains of it then is a figure in a ledger. Some of my capital was employed in the late war; and this country has still my name written down as the proprietor of the capital they blew to pieces in that war.

Having said that for your instruction, let us come down to facts. Mr. Chesterton has formed the Distributist League which organized this meeting. What was the very first thing the League said must be done? It said the coal-mines must be nationalized. Instead of saying that the miner's means of production must be made his own property, it was forced to advocate making national property of the coal-mines. These coal-mines, when nationalized, will not be managed by the House of Commons: if they were you would very soon have no coal. But neither will they be managed by the miners. If you ask the man working in the mine to manage the mine he will say, "Not me, governor! That is your job."

I would like Mr. Chesterton to consider

DO WE AGREE? 29

what he understands by the means of production. He has spoken of them in rather a nineteenth-century manner. He has been talking as though the means of production were machines. I submit to you that the real means of production in this country are men and women, and that consequently you always have the maximum control of the individual over the means of production, because it means self-control over his own person. But he must surrender that control to the manager of the mine because he does not know how to manage it himself. Under the present capitalistic system he has to surrender it to the manager appointed by the proprietors of the mine. Under Socialism he would have to surrender it to the manager appointed by the Coalmaster-General. That would not prevent the product of the mine being equally distributed among the people.

There is no difficulty here. In a sense Mr. Chesterton really does not disagree with me in this matter, since he does see that in the matter of fuel in this country you have to come to nationalisation. Fuel must be controlled equally for the benefit of all the people. Since we agreed upon that, I am not disposed to argue the matter further. Now that Mr. Chesterton agrees that the coal-mines will have to be nationalized he will be led by the same pressure of facts to agree to the nationalization of everything else.

I have to allow for the pressure of facts because, as a playwright, I think of all problems in terms of actual men and women. Mr. Chesterton lets himself idealize them sometimes as virtuous peasant proprietors and self-managing petty capitalists.

The capitalist and the landlord have their own particular ways of robbing the poor; but their legal rights are quite different. It is a very direct way on the part of the landlord. He may do exactly what he likes with the land he owns. If I own a large part of Scotland I can turn the people off the land practically into the sea, or across the sea. I can take women in child-bearing and throw them into the snow and leave them there. That has been done. I can do it for no better reason than that I think it is better to shoot deer on the land than allow people to live on it. They might frighten the deer.

But now compare that with the ownership of my umbrella. As a matter of fact the umbrella I have to-night belongs to my wife; but I think she will permit me to call it mine for the purpose of the debate. Now I have a very limited legal right to the use of that umbrella. I cannot do as I like with it. For instance, certain passages in Mr. Chesterton's speech tempted me to get up and smite him over the head with my umbrella. I may presently feel inclined to smite Mr. Belloc. But should I abuse my right to do what I like with my property—with my umbrella—in this way I should soon be made aware—possibly by Mr. Belloc's fist—that I cannot treat my umbrella as my own property in the way in which a landlord can treat his land. I want to destroy ownership in order that possession and enjoyment may be raised to the highest point in every section of the community. That, I think, is perfectly simple.

There are points on which a landlord, even a Scottish landlord, and his tenant the crofter entirely agree. The landlord objects to being shot at sight. The Irish landlord used to object. His tenants sometimes took no notice of his objection; but all the same they had a very strong objection to being shot themselves. You have no objection to a

State law being carried out vigorously that people shall not shoot one another. There is no difficulty in modern civilized States in having it carried out. If you could once convince the people that inequality of income is a greater social danger than murder, very few people would want to continue to commit it ; and the State could suppress it with the assent of the community generally. We are always adding fresh crimes to the calendar. Why not enact that no person shall live in this community without pulling his weight in the social boat, without producing more than he consumes—because you have to provide for the accumulation of spare money as capital—who does not replace by his own labour what he takes out of the community, who attempts to live idly, as men are proud to live nowadays. Is there any greater difficulty in treating such a parasite as a malefactor, than in treating a murderer as a malefactor?

Having said that much about the property part of the business, I think I have succeeded in establishing that Mr. Chesterton does not disagree with me. I should like to say I do not believe in Democracy. I do believe in

Catholicism; but I hold that the Irish Episcopal Protestant Church, of which I was baptized a member, takes the name of Catholicism in vain ; that the Roman Church has also taken it in vain ; and so with the Greek Church and the rest. My Catholicism is really catholic Catholicism : that is what I believe in, as apart from this voting business and democracy. Does Mr. Chesterton agree with me on that ?

MR. CHESTERTON : Among the bewildering welter of fallacies which Mr. Shaw has just given us, I prefer to deal first with the simplest. When Mr. Shaw refrains from hitting me over the head with his umbrella, the real reason—apart from his real kindness of heart, which makes him tolerant of the humblest of the creatures of God—is not because he does not own his umbrella, but because he does not own my head. As I am still in possession of that imperfect organ, I will proceed to use it to the confutation of some of his other fallacies.

I should like to say now what I ought perhaps to have said earlier in the evening, that we are enormously grateful to Mr. Shaw for his characteristic generosity in consenting to debate with a humble movement like our own. I am so conscious of that condescension on his part that I should feel it a very unfair return to ask him to read any of our potty little literature or cast his eye over our little weekly paper or become conscious of the facts we have stated a thousand times. One of these facts, with which every person who knows us is familiar, is our position with regard to the coal question. We have said again and again that in our human state of society there must be a class of things called exceptions. We admit that upon the whole in the very peculiar case of coal it is desirable and about the best way out of the difficulty that it should be controlled by the officials of the State, just in the same way as postage stamps are controlled. No one says anything else about postage stamps. I cannot imagine that anyone wants to have his own postage stamps, of perhaps more picturesque design and varied colours. I can assure you that Distributists are perfectly sensible and sane people, and they have always recognized that there are institutions in the State in which it is very difficult to apply the principle of individual property, and that one of these cases is the discovery under the earth of valuable minerals. Socialists are not alone in believing this. Charles I, who, I suppose, could not be called a Socialist, pointed out that certain kinds of minerals ought to belong to the State, that is, to the Commons. We have said over and over again that we support the nationalization of the coal-mines, not as a general example of Distribution but as a common-sense admission of an exception. The reason why we make it an exception is because it is not very easy to see how the healthy principle of personal ownership can be applied. If it could we should apply it with the greatest pleasure. We consider personal ownership infinitely more healthy. If there were a way in which a miner could mark out one particular piece of coal and say, "This is mine, and I am proud of it," we should have made an enormous improvement upon State management. There are cases in which it is very difficult to apply the principle, and that is one of them. It is the reverse of the truth for Mr. Shaw to say that the logic of that fact will lead me to the application of the same principle to other cases, like the ownership of the land. One could not illustrate it better than by the case of coal. It may be true for all I know that if you ask a miner if he would like to manage the mine he would say, " I do not want to manage it ; it is for my betters to manage it." I had not noticed that meek and simple manner among miners. I have even heard complaints of the opposite temper in that body. I defy Mr. Shaw to say if you went to the Irish farmers, or the French farmers, or the Serbian or the Dutch farmers, or any of the millions of peasant owners throughout the world, I defy him to say if you went to the farmer and said, "Who controls these farms?" he would say, " It is not for the likes of me to control a farm." Mr. Shaw knows perfectly well it is nonsense to suggest that peasants would talk that way anywhere. It is part of his complaints against peasants that they claim personal possessions. I am not likely to be led to the denial of property in land, for I know ordinary normal people who feel property in land to be normal. I fully agree with Mr. Shaw, and speak as strongly as he would speak, of the abomination and detestable foulness and sin of landlords who drove poor people from their land in Scotland and elsewhere. It is quite true that men in possession of land have committed these crimes; but I do not see why wicked officials under a socialistic state could not commit these crimes. But that has nothing to do with the principle of ownership in land. In fact these very Highland crofters, these very people thus abominably outraged and oppressed, if you asked them what they want would probably say, " I want to own my own croft ; I want to own my own land."

Mr. Shaw's dislike of the landlord is not so much a denial of the right to private property, not so much that he owns the land, but that the landlord has swallowed up private property. In the face of these facts of millions and millions of ordinary human beings who have private property, who know what it is like to own property, I must confess that I am not overwhelmed and crushed by Mr. Shaw's claim that he knows all about men and women as they really are. I think Mr. Shaw knows something about certain kinds of men and women ; though he sometimes makes them a little more amusing than they really are. But I cannot agree with his discovery that peasants do not like peasant property, because I know the reverse is the fact.

Then we come to the general point he raised about the State. He raised a very interesting question. He said that after all the State does command respect, that we all do accept laws even though they are issued by an official group. Up to a point I willingly accept his argument. The Distributist is certainly not an anarchist. He does not believe it would be a good thing if there were no such laws. But the reason why most of these laws are accepted is because they correspond with the common conscience of mankind. Mr. Shaw and Bishop Barnes might think it would be an inadequate way of explaining it, but we might call attention to an Hebraic code called the Ten Commandments. They do, I think, correspond pretty roughly to the moral code of every religion that is at all sane. These all reverence certain ideas about " Thou shalt not kill." They all have a reverence for the commandment which says, " Thou shalt not covet thy neighbour's goods." They reverence the idea that you must not covet his house or his ox or his ass. It should be noted, too, that besides forbidding us to covet our neighbour's property, this commandment also implies that every man has a right to own some property

DO WE AGREE? 39

Mr. Shaw: I now want to ask Mr. Chesterton why he insists, on the point about the nationalization of the coal-mines—on which he agrees with me—that they are an exception. Are they an exception? In what way are the coal-mines an exception? What is the fundamental reason why you must nationalize your coal-mine? The reason is this. If you will go up to the constituency of Mr. Sidney Webb, to the Sunderland coast, you will be able to pick up coal for nothing, absolutely nothing at all. You see people doing it there. You take a perambulator, or barrow, or simple sack, and when the tide goes out you go out on the foreshore and pick up excellent coal. If you go to other parts of England, like Whitehaven, you will find you have to go through workings driven out under the sea, which took 20 years to make, 20 years continual expenditure of capital before coal could be touched, where men going down the shaft have to travel sometimes two or three miles to their work. That is the reason at bottom why you cannot distribute your coal-mine. The reason you have to pay such monstrous prices for your coal is they are fixed by the cost of making the submarine mines. People who have mines like the Sunderland foreshore naturally make colossal fortunes. Everyone can see at once that in order to have any kind of equable dealing in coal, the only way is to charge the citizens the average cost for the total national supply. You cannot average the cost by putting your eggs into different baskets. Now this is not the exception: it is the rule. You have exactly the same difference in the case of the land. You have land worth absolutely nothing at all and land worth a million an acre or more. And the acre worth more than a million and the acre worth nothing are within half-an-hour's drive in a taxi.

You cannot say that the coal-mine is an exception. The coal-mine is only one instance. Mr. Chesterton in arriving at the necessity for the nationalization of the coal-mines has started on his journey towards the nationalization of all the industries. If he goes on to the land, and from the land to the factory, and from there to every other industrial department, he will find that every successive case is an exception; and eventually he will have to say to himself: " I think it will be better to call nationaliza-

DO WE AGREE? 41

tion the rule rather than the exception."

I must deny that I ever said that the coal-miner says he wants to be ruled by his betters. I may not be a democrat; but I am not a snob. Intellectually I am a snob, and you will admit that I have good ground for that. Socially I am not a snob. There is no question of betters at all in the matter. The manager is not better than the executant, nor the executant better than the manager. Both are equally necessary and equally honorable. But if you ask the executant to manage he will refuse on the ground that it is not his job; and vice versa.

Mr. Chesterton says he does not see why State officials under a system which recognises nationalisation of land should not act as the old landlords acted. I should say, in the first place, they won't have the power. A State official does what he is instructed to do and paid to do, just as a landlord's agent does; and there is no more danger of the official making himself a landlord than there is now of the agent making himself one.

As to the instinct of owning—and you have it widely in the country—you have not got it in the towns. People are content to live in houses they do not own : when they possess them they often find them a great nuisance. But you must not conclude that because a miner would refuse to manage a mine a farmer will refuse to manage his farm. The farmer is himself a manager.

How does this wonderful system of peasant proprietorship work ? Do you realise that it has to be broken up every day ? The reason is that when a man owning a farm has a family, each son, when the farmer dies, has a right to an equal part of the land. They find that this arrangement is entirely impossible, and they have to make some other arrangement, and some of the sons have to go off into the towns to work. It is unthinkable that all could remain on the land : you cannot split up the land and give every person a bit of property.

I have stolen two minutes from Mr. Chesterton, and I apologise.

MR. CHESTERTON : I am sure Mr. Shaw is very welcome to as many minutes as I can offer him, or anything else, for his kindness in entertaining us this evening. It is rather late now and there is not much time left for me. He has been rather slow in discovering

DO WE AGREE?

what Distributism is and what the whole question is about. If this were the beginning of the discussion I could go over our system completely. I could tell him exactly what we think about property in towns. It is absurd to say it does not exist.

In rural ownership different problems have to be faced. We are not cutting a thing up into mathematical squares. We are trying to deal with human beings, creatures quite outside the purview of Mr. Shaw and his political philosophy. We know town people are a little different from country people; business of one kind is different from business of another kind; difficulties arise about family, and all the rest of it. We show man's irrepressible desire to own property and because some landlords have been cruel, it is no use talking of abolishing, denying, and destroying property, saying no one shall have any property at all. It is characteristic of his school, of his age. The morality he represents is, above all, the morality of negations. Just as it says you must not drink wine at all as the only solution to a few people drinking too much: just as it would say you must not touch meat or smoke tobacco at all. Let us always remember, therefore, that when Mr.

Shaw says he can persuade all men to give up the sentiment of private property, it is in exactly the same hopeful spirit that he says he will get all of you to give up meat, tobacco, beer, and a vast number of other things. He will not do anything of the sort and I suspect he himself suspects by this time that he will not do it. It is quite false to say you must have a centralised machinery, even in towns. It is quite false to say that all forces must be used, as they are in monopolies, from the centre. It is absurd to say that because the wind is a central thing you cannot separate windmills. How am I to explain all that in five minutes? I could go through a vast number of fallacies into which he has fallen. He said, ironically, he would like to see me go down a mine. I have no difficulty in imagining myself sinking in such a fashion in any geological deposit. I really should like to see him doing work on a farm, because he would find out about five hundred pieces of nonsense he has been speaking to be the nonsense they are.

It is absolutely fallacious to suggest that there is some sort of difficulty in peasantries whereby they are bound to disappear. The answer to that is that they have not disappeared. It is part of the very case against

DO WE AGREE? 45

peasantry, among those who do not like them, that they are antiquated, covered with hoary superstition. Why have they remained through all these centuries, if they must immediately break up and become impossible ? There is an answer to all that and I am quite prepared to give it at some greater length than five minutes. But at no time did I say that we must make the whole community a community of agricultural peasants. It is absurd. What I said was that a desire for property which is universal, everywhere, does appear in a perfect and working example in the ownership of land. It only remains for me to say one thing. Mr. Shaw said, in reference to the State owning the means of production, that men and women are the only means of production. I quite accept the parallel of the phrase. His proposition is that the government, the officials of the State, should own the men and women : in other words that the men and women should be slaves.

MR. BELLOC : I was told when I accepted this onerous office that I was to sum up. I shall do nothing of the sort. In a very few years from now this debate will be antiquated. I will now recite you a poem :

"Our civilization
   Is built upon coal.
Let us chaunt in rotation
Our civilization
That lump of damnation
   Without any soul,
Our civilization
   Is built upon coal.

" In a very few years
   It will float upon oil.
Then give three hearty cheers,
In a very few years
We shall mop up our tears
   And have done with our toil.
In a very few years
   It will float upon oil."

． ． ． ． ． ．

In I do not know how many years—five, ten, twenty—this debate will be as antiquated as crinolines are. I am surprised that neither of the two speakers pointed out that one of three things is going to happen. One of three things : not one of two. It is always one of three things. This industrial civilization which, thank God, oppresses only the small part of the world in which we are most inextricably bound up, will break down and therefore end from its monstrous wickedness, folly, ineptitude, leading to a restoration of sane, ordinary human affairs, complicated but based as a whole upon the freedom of the citizens. Or it will break down and lead to nothing but a desert. Or it will lead the mass of men to become contented slaves, with a few rich men controlling them. Take your choice. You will all be dead before any of the three things comes off. One of the three things is going to happen, or a mixture of two, or possibly a mixture of the three combined.

END